The challenge of communi[cating] ... post-Christian generation can be complex and daunting. Amandola has developed an excellent resource for this specific task. *Foundations: Ancient Faith for Modern People* is creative, theologically and educationally astute, and very practical. It deserves wide usage in the church. I will be recommending it to my own church and to my seminary students.

> Steve Tracy, Ph.D., Professor of Theology and Ethics, Phoenix Seminary; Founder and President, Mending the Soul Ministries

The entirety of this work embodies the essence of grace by giving the audience permission to discover God without the turn-offs of forced outcomes. It allows us to move beyond our false narratives, broken pasts, and judgement of the church. It's safe and it's better than good; it's Good News in a way that gets me.

> Gavin Linderman, Lead Pastor, Axiom Church, Peoria, AZ

This is a marvelous work that is as comprehensive and true as it is accessible to the inquiring mind. Honest exploration of the way of Jesus is the fruit of this resource and I heartily recommend it for anyone seeking to arrive at truth rather than being told what to believe.

> Dr. Geoffrey Hsu, Executive Director, Flourish San Diego

A beautiful and concisely written approach that does not separate body from soul, the material from the immaterial, or the secular from the sacred. This is a holistic view of the gospel that has implications not only in eternity but in the here and now.

> Rev. Paul R. Madson, President, Global Training Network

I love the way John invites the seeker or new believer into the inquiry of the Christian faith. Typically complex inward struggles are allowed free expression within a solid framework of orthodoxy. I believe this book could be a game changer to those wanting to lead others into spiritual, biblical dialogue.

Rev. Jeff Peterson, Director of Pastoral Care
Arizona Network—Assemblies of God

Amandola provides freshness and vibrancy to what it means to gather and learn as a community. The relevance of Scripture combined with practical application makes this not just a valuable resource, but a model for how a community of Christ followers can share their lives together.

Sterling Edwards, Director of Church Planting
Metropolitan New York Baptist Association

John Amandola has done all of those who care about biblically grounded education and discipleship a huge favor by writing *Foundations: Ancient Faith for Modern People*. I'm encouraged by his holistic approach to the faith that touches on eternity while taking the present seriously. The potential applications for this book are endless. From small group study to ministry training curriculum, *Foundations* will serve the Church well for many years to come.

Bryan K. Fergus, M.Div., President, Mission Bible Institute
Adjunct Professor, Phoenix Seminary
Assistant Pastor, Calvary Community Church, Phoenix, AZ

Pastor John Amandola has written a concise, helpful resource for groups of new Christians to discover together the basics of following Jesus. John masterfully weaves biblical truth with holistic personal and corporate application. Although best used in small group settings, any Christian, young or old in the faith, can benefit from walking devotionally through this book.

Terry Coy, Ph.D.
Dean, School of Theological Studies, Missional University

Appreciating the *process* of coming to faith and growing in Christ, *Foundations: Ancient Faith for Modern People* encourages open and honest discussion rather than pressing for agreement. Presenting the truth of the Gospel, allowing participants to freely wrestle with it, and relying on the Holy Spirit to do the teaching, respects both God and those who need to know Him. Having served as an adult small groups pastor I appreciate and endorse John's approach!

Bill Galipault, D.Min.
Sports Ministry Director, Missionary Athletes International

Amandola takes complex concepts and makes them simple to comprehend without diminishing their meanings. This book offers a fresh approach to learning in community that gives learners a voice and the Holy Spirit freedom.

Dr. Norm Wakefield
Professor Emeritus, Phoenix Seminary

John Amandola has given us an excellent approach for engaging with a wide range of people. He shows how to trust the Holy Spirit, pay attention to doctrine, and, at the same time, respect the dignity of everyone. He demonstrates what it is to engage millennials while including all age groups. His understanding of the *Missio Dei* is rich and easily applicable to all Christians. The discussion questions are crafted with precision and respect for everyone participating. I am looking forward to using it in the church I serve where I anticipate some wonderful results.

The Rev. Dr. John F. Maher, Jr.
Vicar, St. Francis Episcopal Church, Manakin Sabot, VA

Being a father of three teenagers as well as working as an undergrad professor who spends hours every week with Millennials, I was eager to dive into this book once I understood that it was about communicating biblical doctrine to Millennials. I've wrestled with the best way to communicate my faith, and in particular theology, to my boys and students that is contextualized to our lives here in post-everything Portland, Oregon. Having been educated in theology from a highly Modernistic worldview, I understand that much of that framework was contextualized for that era and cultural milieu. But what about today? How is biblical doctrine communicated in a contextual manner? That's why I'm appreciative of John Amandola's book. It is a great tool to communicate timeless truth designed for Millennials.

Dr. Sean Benesh
Author, Professor, and Church Planting Strategist

Uniquely designed for Millennials, this book invites each voice to be heard as the readers seek truth in community. Wherever you are in your spiritual journey, find a few peers, walk through this book together, and discover (or re-discover) how intriguing the person of Jesus is, and how transformative the whole gospel can be for every generation from X to Z.

Jeff Getz, Regional Director
The Eastern Region of the Missionary Church

FOUNDATIONS:
Ancient Faith for Modern People

Whole Life Series, Book One

John Amandola, Jr.

MISSIONAL
UNIVERSITY PRESS
SERVICE IN THE MISSION OF GOD

Published by Missional University Press
North Augusta, South Carolina, USA
missional.university/mup

FOUNDATIONS: Ancient Faith for Modern People

ISBN: 978-1-932854-00-8
Library of Congress Control Number: 2016921269

Cover Design: Sherry Varughese
Interior Design: Missional University Press

Printed in the United States of America
First Edition: April 2017

Dedicated to Matthew, Mark, and Hannah,
whose patient and generous voices of wisdom
shared around our kitchen table taught me to understand
and appreciate the hearts and minds of today's
young adult followers of Jesus.

Table of Contents

A Word to Group Leaders

Today's learner does not want to be led into discovery of a predetermined point of view. Discussion questions that solicit obvious answers and "fill-in-the-blank" lessons cause young adults to feel robbed of their voices and manipulated into the opinion of the authority figure. Instead, they greatly appreciate when a leader directly proposes a point of view at the start, and then allows time for free interaction around it in a safe and respectful environment. They want to be free to agree, disagree, cite examples, or propose alternatives in an open and honest exchange of ideas.

In order to create such an environment, we must be willing to release control and trust The Holy Spirit in our midst as we give our students a voice. This is consistent with Luther's teaching on the priesthood of every believer, which tells us that all followers of Jesus have direct access to God. As we gather in community, we trust that The Holy Spirit is working in and through all believers present, empowering them to be givers and receivers of God's grace. Furthermore, those learners present who don't follow Jesus will consequently benefit from the grace present in the community.

Some leaders worry that this style will give them less control over outcomes. They are correct! We simply can no longer expect to effectively relate to our audience while simultaneously maintaining tight control over outcomes. We can *and should* control the viewpoints we propose, but we can't control whether or not people will agree with us. As we humbly release our expectation to control outcomes, we demonstrate both trust in The Holy Spirit and respect for our learners.

This book is meant to be read aloud in small groups. We suggest gathering weekly, having some food, and spending an hour or so in this study. Simply sit in a circle, open the book together, and take turns reading paragraph by paragraph, pausing to answer the discussion questions. Since no set of questions will relate to every audience, it might be beneficial for you to familiarize yourself with the questions beforehand so you can effectively restate them, if necessary, in a way that speaks to the needs and culture of your particular group. Other than that, no preparation is required. Also, you probably won't have time to answer all of the questions, so feel free to skip around as the conversation flows. Remember, it is The Holy Spirit's job to teach. Your role is to facilitate an environment where all group members have a voice and feel heard. Here are a few suggestions for you toward this goal:

Affirm: A fundamental assumption of this study is that Christian leaders ought to meet people wherever they are in their spiritual journey and allow them to progress at their own pace. Therefore, we encourage you to strive to create a learning environment that validates whatever point of view a person has. Validation does not mean to agree, but to grant respect. Therefore, we must always be gracious and thank people for using their voices. It is completely acceptable for you to respectfully disagree and to state your or your church's position. Do not, however, try to debate or persuade people to accept your convictions. Instead, trust that God will reveal his truth in his timing to everyone present, including you! This gives you credibility and motivates people to return and to invite others. Examples of affirming statements are "I appreciate your honesty. Thank you for sharing that," "I can understand why you would feel that way," and "Although we disagree, I respect your point of view and thank you for taking a risk to share it."

Do Not Dominate the Discussion: Your task is simply to ask the questions and wait. Please resist the temptation to fill in the silence. Allow people the time they need to think about the material. Consider using the "9-second rule," waiting at least that long after asking a question before you speak. When you do speak, don't answer the question, but look for a way to rephrase it and then wait again. In the rare case that no one responds again, ask them what they feel the difficulty is with this particular question. If a group member asks for an explanation of something in the material, consider redirecting the question to the other group members rather than answering it yourself. Be frugal with your opinions; if you say too much, you will reinforce to them that only your voice counts.

Ask Follow-Up Questions: These questions ask the learner to explain further or deeper. These must be used very carefully, as not to put someone on the spot. Therefore, it is important to have a strong rapport with people before engaging on this level. Follow-up questions contribute to a beneficial learning environment because they validate responses, encourage participation, and help others learn. Examples of follow-up questions are "Can you tell us why you feel that way?" and "That's great! Can you give me an example of what you mean?"

Avoid Closed-Ended Questions: Nothing derails a conversation more than questions that require only a "yes" or "no" in response. For example, "Do you agree?" Also, try to avoid questions that have only one correct answer. These are usually based on the article and resemble a reading comprehension question on a standardized test. For example, "How many persons did the chapter say are in the Trinity?" These shut down conversation and produce an unsafe environment because people will either fear getting the answer wrong, or they will begin to suspect that you are trying to lead them to a predetermined point of view. Instead, try to rephrase questions to have *no incorrect answers*: "Please share your point of view." You might also rephrase it to have *many correct answers*: "What are some of the implications of that approach?"

Finally, you might notice that there are very few Bible verses quoted. This is not at all to diminish the importance of scripture. Quite the contrary, it is because the purpose of this study is to present an overall biblical theology. Providing verse references here and there in this type of study usually does little to add to credibility and instead teaches learners to "proof text." It is our hope that once a learner understands the overarching message of scripture they will be more equipped to read individual passages in context.

> Your co-laborer,
> John

Introduction

It is common knowledge that young people are leaving churches in large numbers. This does not mean, however, that Millennials are spiritually disinterested. Quite the contrary, they are arguably even more spiritually-minded than their Baby Boomer and Gen X predecessors. So why the departure? As I have taken the time to listen, I have found that many Millennials are not satisfied with modern expressions of church ministry, which they view to be disembodied, disconnected, and individualistic. They long for a holistic faith that does not divorce the secular from sacred, seeks justice for all, is ethnically inclusive, and is fleshed out in everyday life experience. In response to these longings, our little church plant has strived to provide an environment that affirms the goodness of the physical realm, is connected to everyday life and struggles, is intentionally racially diverse, and is contextualized in community. As we have done so, we have experienced much growth with people under thirty years old.

When we began to seek out curriculum to help our people learn the gospel and basic Bible doctrine, we found that most of the available material was a product of previous generations. The purpose of this book, therefore, is to communicate the timeless truths of biblical doctrine in a manner that speaks effectively to the next generation while not excluding previous ones. In fact, it is our hope that this study will help people of all age groups discover or rediscover the gospel and biblical doctrine in a way that gives life to them every day.

While writing this book, we strived to be orthodox, holistic, and full of grace and truth. Since the purpose of doctrine is to know and love God, we also took great care to view theology through the lens of the gospel. Finally, we made every effort to be conscious of the existence of other ancient creation accounts and of modern scientific discoveries, treating them with honesty and respect, rather than as adversaries.

The format of these lessons is intended to facilitate learning in community. We encourage you to read the chapters aloud together and then respond to the readings through interactive discussion. You don't have to know anything in advance to join in the conversation. We are more interested in *what you think* and *how you feel* about the material presented than we are about persuading you to conform to our beliefs. You are welcome to join the discussion and lend your voice no matter what your beliefs are, and you can be assured that your point of view will be respected. If you would prefer not to join the discussion and simply listen, you are more than welcome to learn in that manner as well.

We will generally take turns reading a paragraph at a time. If you prefer not to read aloud, simply say "pass," and the next person will know it is his or her turn. As you read the material, please underline any points that you wish to bring up later. This can be something that is especially meaningful or significant to you, something with which you agree or disagree, or something that needs further explanation. We will always take time to discuss the things that you underline.

We also need to mention a few words about style. First, although we realize that God does not have gender, this study will follow the pattern used in the Bible and employ the male pronoun for God. This is not to say that male is deemed more significant or valuable than female. It is simply a function of the limitations of the English language, which does not have a commonly used gender-neutral personal pronoun. Second, when referring to God's people, we will use first person plural pronouns such as "us" and "we." This is also for simplicity's sake, and not at all to assume that all people using this book consider themselves to be followers of Jesus. We are not intending to exclude anyone. Quite the contrary, we hope to invite you into deeper consideration of the person of Jesus and meet you wherever you are in your spiritual journey.

Finally, we are not attempting to give a comprehensive explanation of Christian beliefs, but a brief overview. Therefore, we expect that this study will leave you with many unanswered questions, perhaps even more than when you started! If this becomes true of you, then we consider ourselves successful in this endeavor, since we believe one gains wisdom by asking questions. Learning is a lifelong pursuit; we only hope to provide a stepping stone for your journey. At the end of each chapter, therefore, we will suggest some Bible passages to read for further study. In many cases, the material in the chapter was in part derived from the teachings of these passages. In all cases, these passages represent just the tip of the iceberg!

Grateful to walk with you,
John

Chapter One: God

"We are lovable precisely because God loves us."
–Desmond Tutu

To support his friend Kristin, Robert decided to attend her grandmother's funeral. This was the first time he had been in a church since he was a kid. "Thanks for coming, Robert. I hope that wasn't too weird for you."

"Glad to be there with you. Your grandmother seemed like an amazing person! But yes, since you asked, it was a bit weird."

"I figured," Kristin replied. "Which parts of the service were strange to you?"

"Mostly the pastor's speech. He talked about God as an actual being who has a consciousness and knows things – like the exact day your grandmother was going to die."

"Are you an atheist then?" Robert had to think about that for a second. "Well, I'm not sure, but if there is a God, I don't think he is like how the pastor described. I believe God might be more like positive energy in the universe that comes from all life."

1. Recent studies have revealed that an increasing number of young people today do not believe in the existence of God. Why do you personally think this

might be so? What are some common reasons people have for doubting that God exists?

2. What are the different ways that an average person who believes in God might describe him?

> *Please read the article below, underlining any points that you wish to bring up later. This can be something that is especially meaningful or significant to you, something with which you agree or disagree, or something that needs further explanation.*

As humans, we can only describe any given entity from our own point of reference. Since our point of reference exists within the physical universe, and since God is not limited to the physical universe, we will never arrive at an adequate description of God. We can, however, know true things *about God*, even though we will never fully understand him. In this chapter, we will describe some things that Christians believe to be true about God's nature and discuss how they relate to our lives today.

God's Incommunicable Attributes

These are characteristics of God that only God possesses; we as humans do not share them. Traditionally, we categorize them as follows: God is *omnipotent*, meaning he is all-powerful; God is *omnipresent*, meaning he is not bound by the limits of space; God is *omniscient*, meaning that he is all-knowing; and God is *eternal*, meaning that he existed in eternity past and will exist in eternity future.

Although these terms are correct, they reflect an older scientific understanding of the universe. For example, we now know that time and space are not separate, but inextricably interrelated. We have also learned that space is more than simply the relative distance between objects. Therefore, the notion of "eternity past" no longer reflects a scientifically sound understanding of the nature of time, which is now known to have a beginning that corresponds with the creation of space.

Given our growing scientific knowledge, it may be more useful to simply say that God is *extracosmic*. The prefix *extra* means "beyond," and *cosmos* is the Greek word for the order of the universe. Therefore, God is not bound by the nature or limits of the physical universe. He exists independent of it, meaning that he is not subject to its properties or laws, whether they are known by humans or yet to be discovered. Although God is not bound by the physical universe, he is not separate from it either. As we will discuss in later chapters, God is near, ever-present, and knowable. Furthermore, he is neither provable nor disprovable by science, since it can only observe and predict phenomena within the material universe.

God is extracosmic because he is the creator, meaning that by his will the universe and all it contains came into being and exists. This is not to say that he created the universe in its present form. It is well within the prerogative of God to create and sustain a dynamic, ever-changing universe. Since he is the creator, creation is absolutely subject to him. It cannot exert any force upon him that might change him and he knows all things within it.

Since God is extracosmic, he is self-existent. This means that he requires only himself and is not dependent on anything he has created. Although he loves and engages with humanity, he does not need anything from us for his own well-being or the implementation of his will.

God's Communicable Attributes

Communicable attributes are characteristics of God that he has *communicated*, or shared, with humans. Of course, the following list is not exhaustive and only reflects our limited understanding of God's nature. *God is love*: We do not say "God is loving," because love is his very nature. Therefore, love predates the universe. God is eternally demonstrating love, both within himself and towards creation. Love was God's primary motivation to create the universe and humanity. *God is holy*: God is morally perfect. His nature is the standard of righteousness and basis of ethics in the universe. *God is just*: God's rule is entirely righteous. The administration of his government is perfect, dispensing mercy, provision, protection, and judgment in a manner perfectly consistent with his love. *God is faithful*: God is absolutely trustworthy and reliable; he will always keep his promises and act consistently with his attributes. *God is personal*: Although spirit, God is not an impersonal force, but a relational being. He can know and be known.

God perfectly displays all of these communicable attributes. As human beings made in his image, these characteristics will become increasingly evident in us as the gospel works in our lives to transform us. Therefore, to be fully human means to become a unique expression of God's love to the world.

The Community of the Trinity

St. Augustine taught us that in order for love to be present, there must be a lover and one who is loved. Love cannot exist without plurality. God is love because he eternally loves within the community of the Trinity.

The doctrine of the Trinity states that God exists as one God in three distinct persons – God The Father, God The Son, and God The Holy Spirit – eternally enjoying perfect relationship with each other. God's relational nature is the foundation for humanity's relational nature and is the reason why the Christian gospel is so unique among world religions. The good news flows from God's love, which motivates him to pursue and restore intimate relationship with humanity.

The doctrine of the Trinity was officially accepted by the worldwide Christian community in the fourth century. Some people use the late acceptance of the doctrine to challenge its validity. It is important to understand, however, that although it is true that this doctrine was not finalized until the fourth century, it is also true that the three points of which this doctrine is comprised were all considered to be true as early as the first century. They were only later compiled together as one doctrine. Let's briefly summarize these three points:

1. God Exists in Three Distinct Persons: Persons are said to possess at least three qualities: *intellect*, our ability to think; *emotions*, our ability to feel; and *volition*, our ability to choose. Thoughts, feelings, and choices are part of what defines a person as unique. Within the Trinity, each person is self-aware, possessing his own thoughts, feelings, and choices. Therefore, the persons of the Trinity are distinct from each other in that the person of

The Son is not the person of The Holy Spirit, The Father is not The Son, and so on. Furthermore, they each carry out distinct roles in the implementation of the gospel. Although *distinct* persons, they are not *separate*, but are unified as one God.

2. Each Person Is Fully God: Each person of the Trinity possesses all the attributes of God, both communicable and incommunicable. Some people have the misconception that because there are examples of The Son yielding his will to The Father's, The Father is more important or more divine than The Son. This, however, is not evidence of a greater degree of importance, but a function of loving, mutual submission and unity of purpose within the Trinity. All three persons are equal both in divinity and importance. Therefore, The Father is God, The Son is God, and The Holy Spirit is God. All are extracosmic, all are love, and all are worthy of worship.

3. God Is One: Christianity is a monotheistic religion, meaning that Christians worship one God. When we say "in three persons," we are not saying that we worship three gods. Each of the three persons is *distinct*, but they are not *separate*. Their unity is more than a oneness of *purpose*, it is a oneness of *being*. God is three persons in one being.

As we said at the beginning of the chapter, since our perspective exists within the physical universe, we can never arrive at an adequate understanding of God, who exists apart from the limits of the physical universe. Therefore, the doctrine of the Trinity is a grand and beautiful mystery. Although it may not reveal his full nature, it does magnificently reveal his bottomless love, which he lavished upon all creation. His love is the very reason the gospel exists. The mission of God flows from the love of God. Since God's very nature is love, he is compelled within himself to redeem creation.

Summary

- Although we will never be able to completely understand God, we can know true things about him.
- Incommunicable attributes are characteristics that God alone possesses.
- God is extracosmic, meaning that he is not bound by the limits or subject to the properties of the material universe.
- God is extracosmic because he is the creator. All that exists came into being and continues to exist by his will.
- Extracosmic does not mean that God is separate from creation. God is also near and knowable.
- God's communicable attributes are qualities that he shares with humans. Among them are *God is love, holy, just, faithful,* and *personal.*
- Love predates creation because it is the very nature of the creator. Therefore, the relationships within the Trinity are the source of love in the universe.
- The three truths that make up the doctrine of the Trinity have always been accepted by Christians: God is three distinct persons, each person is fully God, and God is one.

For Discussion

Please be sure to listen intently without interrupting and ask each other questions in order to gain understanding. Respond with validation, even when disagreeing. At all times strive to maintain respect for one another's point of view.

1. Please take some time as a group to share and discuss what you underlined and why.
2. What are your thoughts and feelings regarding the notion that God is extracosmic? Do you find this to be a useful description? Why or why not?
3. How does the notion that God can't be proved nor disproved by science inform how you consider the question of the existence of God?
4. Which of God's communicable attributes would you like to see more present in humanity and why?
5. How does the concept of love as God's nature compare with our culture's understanding of love?
6. Should the notion that the doctrine of the Trinity is a mystery detract from its credibility in our culture? Why or why not?
7. How can we begin to reconcile the claim that God is love with the fact that there is suffering and hurt in the world?

For Further Study

- Psalm 139: A poem in which the author marvels at the vastness of God's love and thoughts towards humanity.

- Mark 14:32–42: A historical account of Jesus' passionate prayer before his crucifixion. It demonstrates that he has a distinct intellect, emotions, and will from The Father, as well as a unified purpose with The Father.

Chapter Two: Eden

"Life and wisdom are possessed by God, and they are made available to humans as they are in relationship with him. The trouble comes when humans try to seize wisdom on their own terms." –John Walton

Donna finished college several years ago with a degree in marketing and landed her dream job in a large fashion house. She also has a serious and promising relationship with Andrew, whom she met at a party a year ago and with whom she has much in common. Being so far ahead in accomplishing her goals for her age, Donna has the admiration of her many friends. Donna, however, is not so sure it is deserved. She agrees that things are going well, but she still feels a bit empty, as if there is something else she is meant to do, but it is eluding her. So she awakens every morning and goes to work, trying to do her best and make the most out of her life.

1. What are some common avenues people pursue to seek fulfillment in their lives? Where do people search for meaning?
2. In what ways, if any, can you personally identify with Donna's struggle?

> *Please read the article below, underlining any points that you wish to bring up later. This can be something that is especially meaningful or significant to you, something with which you agree or disagree, or something that needs further explanation.*

The word "gospel" means good news. We will see in later chapters that among other things, the Christian gospel results in human beings rediscovering our meaning and purpose in life. In order to rediscover something, we must first understand how it was lost. So that we can fully appreciate the good news of the Christian message, we must first understand the bad news. In the Christian gospel, the bad news is the loss of Eden. In this chapter, therefore, we will go back to the beginning. In the first book in the Bible, Genesis, the author provides us with a rich narrative that reveals to us our original purpose in the Garden of Eden and how it was lost.

Creation

We will discuss in later chapters how to interpret the Bible, but for now it is important to know that the Creation story is first and foremost a story about *why* God created the world, and is not particularly concerned with the sequence or details regarding *how* God created the world. The Creation story is inspired by God to communicate the *meaning* of Creation, not the *manner* of Creation. And the meaning of Creation is this: God spread out the heavens and the earth as his dwelling place and within it created humans as his co-workers and friends. The universe is the temple of God and humans were created to be the priests who tend to it and keep it.

It is well known that there were other ancient creation stories that existed when the biblical account was written. Although there are many similarities between these stories, there are also significant differences between the biblical account and other ancient creation narratives. Through these differences, the inspired author of Genesis highlights profound, life-giving truths unique to the Bible. For example, in other ancient accounts, gods are distant, aloof, and needy, requiring food *from* humans. In Genesis, however, God is near and knowable, serving humanity by providing food *for* us. In other accounts, humanity plays peripheral, inconsequential roles. In the Bible, humanity is central, empowered to represent God and privileged to enjoy relationship with him. Other creation accounts have gardens for the benefit of gods. In Genesis, God planted a garden on the earth for the benefit of humans called "Eden." This garden represents the place within which humans enjoy God's presence and receive his blessings.

Imago Dei

Imago Dei is Latin for "image of God." Genesis tells us that humans are made in God's image, meaning that we are in many ways like him. Just like other ancient temples contained statues carved in the likenesses of the gods they represented, God gave humans his likeness. God's intention for humanity was to be living, breathing images of him, called to represent him on earth. There are many ways humans were created to resemble God:

Relationship: Since humans are made in God's image, we too are relational in nature, possessing the ability to

33

know and be known. In Eden, we enjoyed peace in our relationship *with God*, relating with him as a friend. Humanity also enjoyed peace in our relationships *with each other*. The author of Genesis wrote that in Eden humans were both naked and unashamed. This paints a picture of human relationships that are vulnerable without injury and intimate without shame. Humans also enjoyed unhindered peace in our relationship *with the earth*. We tended the ground and brought forth an abundance of fruit for humanity without injury to the earth. We managed the environment in a manner that caused plants, animals, and other humans to flourish.

Vocation: As beings made in God's image, he intended for us to represent him by maintaining creation so that it is transformed in a manner consistent with God's character. This means that we were originally tasked with managing creation in order to bring about love, justice, and mercy on earth. Our creative, scientific, mathematical, mechanical, intuitive, and other abilities are a result of being made in God's image and allow us to be productive in our vocation to represent him on earth.

Righteousness: Being without sin, we were free to grow in our display of God's communicable attributes without hindrance. We resembled God as we lived together as a loving, holy, just, and faithful people.

Life and Limits

God supplied humanity with all the resources necessary to represent him as his image bearers. In Eden, he planted the Tree of Life, from which humanity was free to eat. It represents empowerment from God. God supplied life as we carried out our vocation to maintain creation. God also planted the Tree of Knowledge of Good and Evil, from which God forbade humans to eat. This tree represents our limits. Wisdom is from God alone and we are not free to pursue it on our own terms by advancing our own agendas. By establishing this limit, God simultaneously created the possibility that humans would violate it, since as beings made in his image, humans have volition.

Humans were placed in Eden to *represent* God. Instead, we decided that we would rather *replace* him. By eating of the fruit of the Tree of Knowledge of Good and Evil, humanity gave up our God-given vocation and chose instead to pursue wisdom on our own terms. That choice brought about sudden and devastating consequences.

The Effects of Sin

By pursuing wisdom on our own, humanity brought sin into the world. Sin immediately broke the peace in our relationships with God, one another, and the earth. It marred the image of God within us, diminishing our ability to reflect God's communicable attributes. Naked and unashamed were replaced by shame, hiddenness, and violence. Sin also introduced disorder into the cosmos, causing the earth to bring forth fruit only with great labor and sweat, and hindering the advancement of justice and mercy on earth.

The catastrophic results of sin are seen all around us: in our dysfunctional relationships, in unjust political systems that oppress and enslave people, in the declining condition of our environment, in our struggle to find purpose and meaning in our lives, and in our addictions and destructive behaviors. Instead of living in Eden, we live in darkness. Instead of enjoying peace with all things, we now endure conflict.

Sin also brought spiritual death upon humanity. As a result of our pursuit of wisdom on our own terms, God expelled us from Eden, cutting us off from access to the Tree of Life. Spiritual death means that we forfeited God's empowerment to carry out our meaning and purpose on earth. In order to keep us from destroying ourselves as a result of this loss, God introduced the law to protect us, replacing one rule with hundreds. God's law is holy and righteous, but impossible for humans to keep perfectly. Therefore, the law also brought with it more sin, more guilt, and more death.

Humanity's exile from Eden also disconnected us from God's abiding presence. He did not, however, abandon us to live forever without him. Instead, God instructed his people to build a tent, then after that a temple. Within these structures, God indwelled a small room called The Holy of Holies. God graciously provided a High Priest to serve as a mediator between God and his people. Once a year, the High Priest was allowed access to God's holy presence in the Holy of Holies to seek atonement for the sins of God's people.

Hope

The entire Bible is the story of God's work to restore Eden and reconcile our relationships with him, each other, and the earth through Jesus Christ. He is our great High Priest, reestablishing for us access to God's empowerment and abiding presence. This is a story of the redemption of all things, motivated by God's love for humanity. Not only is he working to redeem the entire earth through Jesus Christ, but he is also inviting us along in that work, restoring our meaning and purpose in life as his empowered representatives called to bring about justice and mercy on earth.

Summary

- The Creation story in the Bible is concerned with the purpose of Creation, not the manner in which it came about.
- The purpose of Creation is to be a temple for God, with humans as priests who tend to it and represent him.
- The differences between the Bible and other ancient creation accounts demonstrate the uniqueness of the Christian story.
- Human beings are made in God's image. Therefore, we are like him in many ways:
  - We possess the ability to have relationships.
  - We possess many other special qualities that enable us to carry out our vocation to represent him.
  - We have the ability to share God's communicable attributes.
- God is our only source of life and wisdom.
- Human beings chose to replace God rather than represent him, bringing sin into the cosmos.
- The effects of sin were catastrophic, damaging individuals, human relationships, systems and structures in society, and the environment.
- Since we lost access to our source of empowerment, God gave us the law to protect us.

- Unable to keep the law, we became increasingly guilty before God.
- The entire Bible is the story of how God redeemed the earth from sin and death through Jesus Christ.

For Discussion

Please be sure to listen intently without interrupting and ask each other questions in order to gain understanding. Respond with validation, even when disagreeing. At all times strive to maintain respect for one another's point of view.

1. Please take some time as a group to share and discuss what you underlined and why.
2. In what ways do you suppose an understanding that the Creation story communicates *why*, not *how*, the universe was made might change the way the Bible is valued by skeptical people?
3. How does our original purpose as proposed in Genesis compare and contrast with how many people in our culture view their purpose in life?
4. In what ways are the loss of peace in our relationships with God, each other, and the earth most observable?
5. How does the proposal that God created the possibility of sin when he established a limit for humans inform the conversation regarding the existence of evil and suffering in the world?
6. Given the assertion that spiritual death means forfeiting God's empowerment to carry out our meaning and purpose, what are the implications with respect to finding fulfillment in life?

For Further Study

- Genesis Chapters 1–3: This is the creation narrative, including the account of humanity's decision to replace God rather than represent him.
- Romans 5:12–17: This is a portion of a letter written to the Romans by The Apostle Paul. In this passage, he discusses the relationships between sin, death, and the law.

Chapter Three: The Message and Effects of the Gospel

"Salvation, then, is not 'going to heaven' but 'being raised to life in God's new heaven and new earth.'"
–N.T. Wright

"Why rearrange the deck chairs on the Titanic? It's going down anyway." Brock, a sincere Christian, was insistent that involvement in social justice issues, although admirable, was not the best use of a Christian's time. Thiago, also a sincere Christian, was beginning to feel a bit angry with his friend.

"What about all the racial injustice around us? Should we ignore it?"

"Listen, this world is going to pass away, just like a sinking ship, and meanwhile people are going to hell. Isn't it better if we help as many people as possible get saved into heaven, where there is no more injustice? So let's just give them the gospel." Thiago felt there was something a bit off with Brock's logic but had a difficult time verbalizing it.

1. In what ways do you identify with the viewpoint of Thiago? Of Brock?
2. What do you observe to be the implications of Brock's message in the church? In society?

> *Please read the article below, underlining any points that you wish to bring up later. This can be something that is especially meaningful or significant to you, something with which you agree or disagree, or something that needs further explanation.*

A common viewpoint among Christians is that the world is like a sinking ship and its demise is inevitable. Consequently, the main goal of this kind of faith becomes getting as many people as possible into the "lifeboats" in order to rescue them. From this perspective, "good news" is primarily understood as the offer to be saved out of the unspiritual, physical world into a spiritual and immaterial afterlife. This message is simple: "Jesus died for your sins, so accept him, and you will go to heaven." The incompleteness of this statement, however, effectively disconnects the gospel from both the here and now and from the earth. In this view, the church's mandate to improve the lives of people in our society becomes a diminished priority because it is not understood to be part of the gospel. Therefore, this mindset often validates social justice only if it leads people into making a decision to accept Jesus so that they can go to heaven.

By contrast, in this chapter, we will see that although the message of the gospel includes what happens when we die, it is mostly concerned with what happens in the *here and now*. To explore this, we will take a look at five aspects of the gospel as taught in the Bible – Incarnation, Death, Resurrection, Reign, and Return – and discuss together the results of these truths.

1. Jesus Came

The technical word for this truth is "incarnation," which means "in the flesh." In The Gospel of John, the Apostle writes that Jesus, who is God, "became flesh and made his dwelling among us," and that the person of Jesus reveals to us God's nature and purpose. Jesus was sent by God, walked and talked with his followers, and shared his life with them. As a human, he endured all the same temptations that we experience and understands our weaknesses first-hand.

This good news means that we once again can have relationship with God. We can know God and be known by him, as he originally intended in Eden. In this way, Christianity is unique: God pursues humans and is personal, near, and knowable. He can relate to the human experience. Furthermore, the truth of the incarnation also reveals to us the goodness of the material world. Jesus does not remove us from the material world to meet him, but he enters the material world to meet us. This affirms the goodness of our physical bodies and the earth. Jesus did not come to save us from our bodies or from the earth, but to renew them both through his life.

2. Jesus Died

Because of our sin, God judged us by expelling us from Eden, disconnecting us from life and bringing upon us guilt because of our inability to keep the law. In spite of all the good humanity has accomplished, we still fall short of God's righteousness. Furthermore, the burden of sin enslaves us, keeping us captive under its power. Since, however, God loves us and desires relationship with us, rather than leave us to endure the consequences of our sin, Jesus died for our sins as the ultimate act of love and friendship for us.

This good news means that once again we meet God's standard of righteousness, because Jesus' death breaks the power of sin and rescues us from God's judgment. Our human works can't make us righteous, but Jesus' work can and does. Therefore, through the cross we can receive forgiveness of our sins, reconciliation in our relationship with God, and access to new life. The profound implication of this truth is that God is not rescuing us from a "sinking ship," but from the devastating consequences of our own sin.

3. Jesus Rose from the Dead

Jesus' body did not stay in the grave but was once again filled with life. This is the central truth upon which the Christian faith rests. After he rose, Jesus, in his restored body, walked, talked, and ate with his followers. Through his resurrection, Jesus conquered death and reversed the brokenness brought by sin. The same power that raised Jesus from the dead also now lives in his followers and is at work in and through us, empowering us to again take our place as his representatives. Furthermore, because of Jesus' resurrection, the bodies of God's people will not remain in their graves but will also someday be raised to life.

The good news of the resurrection means that the brokenness brought about by our sin is not permanent. Now, as his followers, we once again can enjoy God's abiding presence as we encounter the life-changing presence of the risen Jesus in community. This means that the gospel is not just for those who don't believe, but it is especially for those who do!

Not only does the power of the resurrected Jesus live in us, it also works through us to bring transformation upon the earth. Eventually, through the power of the risen Christ, the renewal of all things will take place. Both people *and* places will be transformed because he is alive.

4. Jesus Reigns

After Jesus rose from the dead and spent many days with his followers, he ascended into heaven as they watched him disappear into the clouds. Then, he sat at the right hand of God. This means that he took his place upon his throne, from where he now and forever reigns as king, exercising his authority in heaven and upon earth.

This good news means that Jesus is actively working to bring about his kingdom of justice and mercy on earth in the here and now. He is reversing the corrupt systems and brokenness that keep people in darkness. This means that the gospel is good news for the whole earth! It is good news for the poor and oppressed because his kingdom is one where oppressive systems will be made right. It is good news for all the nations because God will reconcile all races and peoples to each other and to God. It is good news for God's people because we are invited to join with him to bring about his kingdom of justice and mercy.

5. Jesus Will Return

The Bible promises that we will see Jesus return to earth in the same manner as his disciples saw him ascend to heaven. Upon his return, all people will be raised from the dead. He will then make all things right in heaven and on earth as he sits as a righteous judge, ridding creation of sin and death once and for all. The eternal state will be a renewed heaven and earth, where God's people will live forever in renewed, physical bodies and reign with our eternal king, Jesus.

Although no one quite understands the details of Jesus' return, we do know that it is good news because God will finish the work he began of redeeming all things on heaven and earth through Jesus. This means that the earth is not a sinking ship with an inevitable demise. More accurately, the earth is like a pregnant mother, waiting to give birth to a new heaven and a new earth. Therefore, the Christian faith is about joining God in bringing about his kingdom in the here and now as we look forward to Jesus establishing it forever in the future.

Summary

- The incarnation means that Jesus came to earth in the flesh and is therefore knowable and can identify with our struggles.
- The incarnation affirms the goodness of the physical universe.
- Jesus died, saving us from the curse of sin.
- Jesus rose from the dead, renewing his presence among his people, and providing us with the power

of God for the transformation of people and places as he lives in and through his people.

- Jesus reigns and therefore exercises his dominion in the here and now to bring about justice and mercy upon the earth.

- Jesus will return someday to raise us from the dead and restore heaven and earth for all eternity.

- The earth is therefore not a "sinking ship," but like a pregnant mother, waiting to give birth to a new heaven and new earth.

- We should work to bring about the Kingdom of God in the here and now as we anticipate it coming to completion in the future.

- Our faith is about God raising us to life onto a renewed heaven and earth.

For Discussion

Please be sure to listen intently without interrupting and ask each other questions in order to gain understanding. Respond with validation, even when disagreeing. At all times strive to maintain respect for one another's point of view.

1. Please take some time as a group to share and discuss what you underlined and why.
2. How does the realization that Christianity affirms the goodness of the material word affect your perspective on faith and life?
3. How is the contrast between the images of a sinking ship and a pregnant mother meaningful to you?

4. Can you give some tangible examples of ways in which you have witnessed God's presence demonstrated in the midst of his people?

5. How does the claim that the gospel is especially for believers compare to how you have heard the gospel relayed in your experience? Why is this claim significant?

6. Given the claim that the resurrection brings transformation to both people and places, can you identify some areas in need of transformation around you? What would that transformation look like?

7. Since the kingdom is in the here and now, as well as in the future, discuss your thoughts on the relationship between the gospel message and engagement in social and environmental justice.

8. How is the view that Jesus' return will bring about renewal to the earth different than what you might have previously heard about "the end times"?

For Further Study

- Isaiah Chapter 1: This is prophetic literature, which is an intensely emotional call to God's people to repent. In this section, the prophet discusses several themes, such as the problem of useless religion and the importance of defending the marginalized.

- Romans 8:18–30: In this portion of Paul's letter, he discusses the relationship between our present struggles and the redemption of all things in the future, employing the metaphor of a pregnant mother.

Chapter Four: Our Response to the Gospel

"Becoming a Christian is much like adopting a new life story…when we are converted, we switch stories, we reenter the plan of God." –Todd Hunter

Guan-yin, who has adopted the English name Gwen, is a graduate student from Beijing who studies accounting at an American university. Being very curious about American culture, she decided to visit the local church that sends a bus to pick students up at her campus. She was very well received and graciously included as part of the church community. As she returned week after week, she became acquainted with the stories of the people around her. In particular, she got to know Anthony, an older gentleman who is also an accountant. He had resigned from his lucrative position because his supervisor pressured him to compromise his integrity. This decision intrigued Gwen.

After church one morning, Anthony and his wife Angela invited Gwen to lunch. During their conversation, Angela asked Gwen what her impressions of church were so far. "Well, Jesus seems to require a lot from his followers. But I have also seen so much transformation in them, so I know that he must be real."

Anthony ventured to ask, "So do you believe in Jesus, too?"

"Well, yes, and I want to become a Christian, but I don't know if I am ready yet."

1. What do you think it means in Gwen's mind to be a Christian? What do you think her hesitation is?
2. How might her understanding of what it means to be a Christian be different than what you may have heard or have been taught?

> *Please read the article below, underlining any points that you wish to bring up later. This can be something that is especially meaningful or significant to you, something with which you agree or disagree, or something that needs further explanation.*

In the previous chapter, we said that the gospel is much more than God providing a "lifeboat" to rescue us from a sinking ship. It follows that our response to the gospel should be more than just making a decision to get into that lifeboat. In fact, we will learn in this chapter that our best response is not at all to *escape*, but to *engage* – to reorient one's life to align with God's redemptive work. Remember, in Eden God intended for us to represent him on earth. We instead chose to replace him and pursue our own story rather than his. So when we decide to follow Jesus, we switch stories and reorient our lives to again take our place as his empowered representatives.

As we respond to each of the five aspects of the good news, we further engage in our lifelong journey of following Jesus. It is important to remember that in every case, God moves first and then we respond to him:

1. Seeking, Our Response to "Jesus Came"

Through his incarnation, Jesus made the invisible God visible. He is the bridge through whom we can once again have relationship with God as we did in Eden. God promises that those who truly seek him will be rewarded and will find him.

Our response is to seek God with a sincere heart. As relational beings, we were created to know and be known by him. This means that we must be vulnerable and willing to allow ourselves to be shaped by our encounter with him. Since authentic relationships require acceptance, we must accept God as we find him. We must not make him in our image by seeking a preconceived version of who we wish to find, accepting the attributes of God that are appealing to us, while rejecting ones that we find less desirable. Many seekers find but ultimately reject God because they are not willing to accept the full implications of who God is and what he will want to do in their lives. Those who seek and find God quickly learn that God desires both to transform us and to work with us towards the transformation of people and places.

2. Faith, Our Response to "Jesus Died"

Since our exile from Eden, the human tendency has always been to replace God by seeking to justify ourselves through our own efforts. Because the standard of righteousness is God himself, even the most sincere people will never meet his standard on their own. Humans will never be able to fully keep the law. Therefore, we need what Martin Luther called an "alien righteousness,"

51

or a righteousness that comes not from ourselves, but from another. God freely and graciously provides this righteousness for us through the cross of Jesus.

We receive the benefit of Jesus' death through faith, meaning simple trust in God. By faith, we receive forgiveness of sin and the righteousness of Christ. We place our dependence on him and his work on the cross, rather than on our own efforts, to become righteous. We trust that by his death he will break the power of sin in our lives and transform us by his Spirit. When we believe in Jesus and his work, we become children of God and enter into eternal life.

3. Repentance, Our Response to "Jesus Rose"

As a result of the resurrection, the same power that raised Jesus to life now lives in God's people. Like in Eden, when humans had access to the Tree of Life, we are now empowered by God to carry out his purpose for us. We are free to live the lives that God intended for us when he created Eden.

We respond to the empowerment of God in our lives by obeying him. This is called repentance, or turning from our sin. Repentance is the other side of faith. When we *turn to* Jesus by faith, we necessarily *turn from* our tendency to write our own stories and pursue wisdom on our own terms. As we seek God's plan for our lives, his power works in and through us to deepen our relationship with him so that we can experience transformation.

Repentance is a work of God's Spirit in us from start to finish. It is by God's Spirit that we are made aware of our sin. We feel a healthy internal shame that causes us to identify areas of sin in our lives and to feel sorry for it.

The Spirit also empowers us to turn from our sin and obey. It is important to remember, however, that obedience does not cause God to accept us. He already accepts us based on Jesus' obedience. It is the power of the resurrection that works within us to make us into new creations.

4. Following, Our Response to "Jesus Reigns"

As king, Jesus has all authority on heaven and earth, and his authority is the basis for our call to mission. Just as God sent Jesus into the world, Jesus is now sending us into the world. In fact, following Jesus means that we are sent by him to engage in his mission. His mission is to bring about the renewal of all things on heaven and earth. Therefore, we respond to the reign of Jesus by engaging with God in his mission.

We can work to bring about the Kingdom of God in the here and now as we anticipate Christ's future return. Whether through evangelism, helping the poor, working to right unjust and oppressive societal structures, or protecting our environment – all these things anticipate what God will complete when Jesus returns.

5. Hoping, Our Response to "Jesus Will Return"

To hope is to be certain that a promise will be fulfilled and to consequently order one's life based on that expectancy. Jesus promised to return to righteously judge the nations, do away with sin and death, and renew all things once and for all. We respond to this promise by placing our hope in the one who will certainly bring it to pass.

Just like the certainty of an approaching finish line motivates an athlete to keep running, our hope in the return of Jesus motivates us to endure, even when we face trials and sufferings. Hope also causes us to be encouraged in the face of injustice, because we know that Jesus is the righteous judge who will make all things right. Because we have hope, we live in obedience and flee evil as we await his return. Since we do not know when that will be, we should strive to be faithful at all times as we depend on his resurrection power that is working in us.

In conclusion, to journey as a follower of Jesus means to continually respond to the gracious works of God towards humanity. As we do so, we deepen our partnership with him as he redeems the world and all that is within it through Jesus Christ.

Summary

- Responding to the gospel means to reorient our lives to once again represent God rather than replace him.
- We respond to the incarnation by seeking God with a sincere heart.
- We respond to the death of Jesus and receive forgiveness of sins by faith, not works.
- We respond to the resurrection power of God in our midst through repentance, turning from our sinful tendency to pursue our own agendas.
- We respond to the reign of Jesus by joining with him in bringing about his kingdom in the here and now.
- We respond to the future return of Jesus by living in anticipation of it, enduring and persevering because we are certain he will keep his promises.

For Discussion

Please be sure to listen intently without interrupting and ask each other questions in order to gain understanding. Respond with validation, even when disagreeing. At all times strive to maintain respect for one another's point of view.

1. Please take some time as a group to share and discuss what you underlined and why.

2. In what ways and through what avenues do people you know commonly seek God?

3. In what ways can you relate to the experience of seeking and finding God but struggling with the willingness to be vulnerable with him?

4. We said that repentance is the other side of faith. How might it look in one's life if one were to separate these two concepts? Do you think it is possible to have faith without repentance? Why or why not?

5. At what point in the journey from seeking to hoping do you suppose one may consider himself a Christian? Why do you think so?

6. Evaluate the following common phrases in light of our discussion: "accepting Jesus into my heart," "getting saved," and "praying to receive Christ."

7. We said that activities like helping the poor and protecting the environment are legitimate responses to the gospel. How is that different than what you have heard in the past? How does this change the way one might view Christianity?

8. In what ways does the promise of Christ's return encourage you? Motivate you?

For Further Study

- Luke 9:18–27: In this historical gospel account, Jesus discusses in part what the implications are of being his follower.
- Ephesians 2:1–10: In this portion of Paul's letter to the believers in Ephesus, he discusses humanity's inability to save ourselves and the necessity of faith in Jesus.

Chapter Five: Humanity, Jesus, and The Holy Spirit

"What a profound thought! Jesus, who was God himself,
experienced all of life just as we do. He did not utilize
his divine power to live out his life on earth.
Yet, he lived a life free of sin." –Dann Spader

Nathan, who started following Jesus a few months ago, began to realize that his use of porn was having some destructive consequences in his life. After a few unsuccessful attempts at quitting, he sought out José, who he remembered from church had the same issue. "Nate, because God made us in his image, we all have a longing for meaningful connection with others. That's why porn is not fulfilling, because our real need is intimacy, which porn doesn't provide."

"Yeah, I get that—but I still have all these feelings. How do I deal with them?"

"I guess in the same way Jesus did, by meeting his need for intimacy as he depended on God. You see—"

"Gotta stop you there, José, that's not a fair comparison. Wasn't Jesus God? So he didn't have this problem!"

"On the contrary, Nate, Jesus was fully human, too. He had all the same needs, temptations, and struggles that all other people do."

"Well, I am not sure if I buy that. It doesn't seem right to say that Jesus would feel this way."

1. Can you identify with Nathan's difficulty in accepting that Jesus had human struggles and weaknesses? Why do you think this is hard for some people to accept?
2. Knowing that Jesus also had human needs and struggles, how does this affect the way you view being human?

Please read the article below, underlining any points that you wish to bring up later. This can be something that is especially meaningful or significant to you, something with which you agree or disagree, or something that needs further explanation.

Sayings such as "to err is human" or "you're only human" are commonly used in our culture to graciously excuse honest mistakes. On a deeper level, however, these phrases seem to communicate that being human is a malady to be cured or a flaw to overcome. Even many Christians believe to become more like Jesus means that their humanity must in some way be diminished. We will see in this lesson, however, that as the gospel works in our lives to make us more like Jesus, we actually become more fully human! In fact, Jesus himself, in being fully human, modeled for us everything that God desires us to be and enjoy as human beings. Therefore, humanity is something to be *reclaimed* through the gospel, not *escaped*. In this chapter, we will explore what it means to be fully human as God intended, and what roles Jesus and The Holy Spirit play in that process.

Humanity

A central truth in the Christian faith is that all human beings are made in the image of God. This means that in many ways we are like God. One important way that we are like him is our capacity to enjoy our creative abilities. Just as God enjoys the fruit of his creativity, so do we. We express the image of God within us when we build bridges, write poetry, analyze spreadsheets, dance, compete in sports, play a blues riff, drive racecars, or design dresses. Being made in his image, we each have a unique way in which we can carry out and enjoy our vocation as God's representatives.

God is also a relational being, existing eternally in interdependent relationship with himself in the Trinity. He made us with a similar relational nature. We have a God-given need for human intimacy. When we love and serve each other, work together towards a common goal, enjoy the company of friends, or even feel lonely, we are functioning as beings made in God's image.

Another important way that we express the image of God within us is by accomplishing our God-given purpose to bring about his kingdom of justice and mercy on earth. That is why God gave us access to his communicable attributes. To be truly and fully human is to be loving, holy, just, and faithful people who reflect God's likeness on earth and join him in his redemptive work.

The problem arose when humanity decided that instead of representing God, we would rather replace him. By eating of the Tree of Knowledge of Good and Evil, we chose to pursue all the good things that God wanted for us, but on our own terms. This is what it means to sin: to bring about our own agenda rather than

God's. Our sinful choice introduced chaos into the cosmos and marred the image of God in humanity. We seek to fulfill our God-given and legitimate needs in destructive ways. We become less loving, holy, just, and faithful. We cause hurt, destruction, and death.

All is not lost, however; even the most sinful person to some extent still reflects the image of God and therefore has inherent dignity and value. Our sin can only, to lesser or greater degrees, distort how clearly his image is expressed through us, but it does not eradicate it.

The intent of the gospel is not to do away with our humanity but to empower us to be our true, authentic selves. Just as one buys a historic home and restores the original hardwood floors, stained glass windows, millwork, etc., in order to retain the home's original character, God too renews us with his life but preserves who we are.

The gospel works in the life of every follower of Jesus to restore our humanity as God intended in Eden. The Christian life is not merely a transaction that happened at some point in one's past. Nor is it merely a promise that is fulfilled after one dies. For the most part, the Christian life is lived out through one's physical body here and now on planet earth! Therefore, one's spiritual growth as a follower of Jesus is a direct effect of the gospel. Jesus and The Holy Spirit play integral roles in accomplishing this redemption in the lives of his followers.

Jesus

The effects of sin inhabit us and surround us. Sin enslaves us under its power, breaks our relationship with God, mars the image of God in all humans, corrupts the earth, and creates unjust political and societal systems. The cross of Christ sets us free from all these effects of sin. Jesus' death accomplishes *reconciliation*, providing forgiveness from the guilt of sin, restoring our broken relationships with God, and reversing the destructive effects of sin on earth. It also accomplishes *liberation*, setting us free from the bondage of sin and breaking the strongholds of unjust systems on earth. Jesus' death also accomplishes *victory*; he conquered death so that we can be released from its power. Now that we are set free from the power of sin and death through the cross, we can begin to reclaim our full humanity as God intended for us in Eden.

Jesus is the ultimate example of what it means to be fully human. As we have already learned, Jesus is fully God, possessing all the incommunicable attributes of God. With The Father and The Holy Spirit, he indeed created the universe and all that is in it. Yet, through his incarnation, Jesus also became human. In being fully human, he was no less God, and in being fully God, he was no less human. As a human being, he was subjected to all the temptations, weaknesses, and limitations that we are, yet lived without sinning. He perfectly displayed all of God's communicable attributes in human flesh, modeling the true and full humanity that was meant for us in Eden. It is important to know that Jesus did not draw upon his powers as God to live out his humanity. He did this in the same way that we are meant to, through dependence on God. In this way, he is truly an example of humanity that we can follow.

The Holy Spirit

When Jesus rose from the dead and sat at God's right hand, God sent The Holy Spirit to us. Being God, The Holy Spirit is personal and possesses all the attributes of God. Many people mistakenly refer to him with an impersonal pronoun such as "it." He, however, is not an impersonal energy force, but God with whom we can have relationship and who is worthy of our worship and obedience. He is near to us and empowers us to become more fully human. The works of The Holy Spirit in one's life can be seen in two main categories: those he initially does when one first believes, and his ongoing works in the lives of followers of Jesus.

Among his initial works in our lives are *Calling:* the work of The Holy Spirit to help us seek, repent, and believe; *Sealing:* marking believers with a sign of God's ownership; *Baptizing:* his work to bring believers into spiritual union with the body of Christ, not to be confused with water baptism; and *Regenerating:* his work of giving followers of Jesus new life.

Among the numerous ongoing works of The Holy Spirit are *Conviction of sin*: making us aware of our sin so we can repent from it; *Encouragement:* helping us to persevere in obedience and faith; *Indwelling:* being present in the church as the agent that causes us to be the Body of Christ on earth; *Filling:* empowering us to trust and obey God; *Illumination:* helping us to understand and apply the Bible; *Intercession:* helping us to pray; *Producing fruit:* transforming us supernaturally to display God's communicable attributes; *Giving gifts:* giving us unique abilities and temperaments that enable us to contribute to the health and wholeness of the church; and *Empowering for mission:* producing supernatural results through our efforts to bring about the Kingdom of God on earth.

In conclusion, God created us in Eden to be fully human and to represent God on earth. Although sin has hindered this process, it has not derailed it! The good news is that through the works of Jesus and The Holy Spirit, God is graciously restoring our humanity.

Summary

- God made humans in his image, so the more we are transformed by the gospel, the more human we become.

- Our sin makes us less human, but does not fully eradicate the image of God in us.

- As the gospel renews us, God preserves our true and unique selves.

- The cross of Jesus provides reconciliation, liberation, and victory.

- Jesus saves us from all the effects of sin, so we become free to be fully human.

- Jesus was fully God and fully human. He had all the same human limitations and weaknesses we do, yet without sin.

- Jesus accomplished his humanity without using his divine power and is therefore an example of living a life of dependence on God.

- The Holy Spirit is not an impersonal force, but fully God, personal and holy.

- The Holy Spirit works in our lives to help us believe, repent, and follow Jesus.

- The Holy Spirit works in our lives on an ongoing basis, transforming us and empowering us to follow Jesus day-to-day.

For Discussion

Please be sure to listen intently without interrupting and ask each other questions in order to gain understanding. Respond with validation, even when disagreeing. At all times strive to maintain respect for one another's point of view.

1. Please take some time as a group to share and discuss what you underlined and why.
2. How does the notion that the intent of the gospel is to make us more human change your thoughts and feelings about Christianity?
3. How does recognizing that you are made in God's image change how you view your life and vocation?
4. Which aspects of being made in God's image are most meaningful to you?
5. How does the fact that Jesus' death broke the power of sin inform your approach when you encounter the effects of sin in society?
6. How does the claim that Jesus accomplished his humanity without using his divine power inform how you view him? Your walk with God?
7. Have you been able to recognize any of the works of The Holy Spirit in your life? Can you give examples? In what ways has he helped you?

For Further Study

- Matthew 4:1–11: In this famous gospel account, Satan attempts to coerce Jesus to use his divine powers to fulfill his humanity rather than depend on The Father.
- Galatians 5:13–26: In this letter from Paul to the Christians in Galatia, he encourages them to live in the power of The Holy Spirit.

Chapter Six: Revelation

"We refuse to hear the million different voices through which God speaks to us, and every refusal hardens us more and more against his grace—and yet he continues to speak to us: and we say He is without mercy!"
–Thomas Merton

"I have no more reason to believe that there is a God than I do to believe that there is a teapot orbiting the sun that is too small to see. Neither can be disproved scientifically, but there is no evidence to support their existence either." Becca, a brilliant software engineer, employed this common argument with her friend Carolyn, a pharmacist and follower of Jesus with whom she grew up. They were catching up after not seeing each other for a few years.

"Becca, you're right, God can't be proved scientifically. Since he exists apart from the material world, and science can only measure the material, he is neither provable nor disprovable by science."

"My point exactly, so why believe in him? Especially since everything we know about physics and biology today disproves the Bible. You're a woman of science, Carolyn, you should know that."

"Becca, this might be new to you, but I take the findings of modern science as authoritative *and* I also believe the Bible is true."

"That sounds like a contradiction to me. How can that be?"

1. Given that science can only measure and predict within the physical universe, what role do you believe it can legitimately play in informing ethics and faith?
2. In what ways are you aware that science and the Bible seem to contradict? What are some solutions to this conflict that you have heard proposed?

Please read the article below, underlining any points that you wish to bring up later. This can be something that is especially meaningful or significant to you, something with which you agree or disagree, or something that needs further explanation.

How does God make himself known? What is the relationship between science and the Bible? What is the nature of truth? How are we to interpret the Bible? In this chapter, we will learn that God has revealed himself in many ways. We will see that the Bible is indeed a reliable source of truth and that we do not have to treat scientific truth as an adversary to our faith. We can enjoy the pursuit of truth in our lives without fear of losing our faith.

General Revelation

A walk on the beach at sunrise, a gaze at the stars on a dark night, the cooing of a newborn as you hold her for the first time. These are moments that are beyond themselves, when the Divine whispers to us. We experience some sense of the eternal and instinctively know that there is some meaning and purpose to our existence beyond survival. Anthropologists tell us that all cultures on earth have some concept of God. This is because God, in his love for us, has made his existence self-evident through the physical universe. This knowledge is called "General Revelation."

Although General Revelation does not tell us everything about God, it does give all human cultures a general awareness of his existence and a religious impulse. Even in our frenzied, technologically advanced society, we can still discipline ourselves to quiet our hearts, attune our senses to our surroundings, and become more aware of the presence of God in our lives and around us. This is the ancient Christian practice of *mindfulness*, to know God through our physical senses and hear his "million different voices."

Mindfulness is not exclusive to Christianity; most major religions teach that one can experience God by becoming more present in the routine experiences of everyday life. This has led many Christians to mistakenly reject this discipline because they believe it to be associated exclusively with other faiths. Many Christians, however, have recently begun to re-engage in this ancient practice and are experiencing God in new and fresh ways.

Specific Revelation

God in his love went beyond revealing his existence to humanity. He also worked to graciously reveal to us his nature, how we can have relationship with him, and our purpose in the universe. This is called "Specific Revelation." This refers to the particular ways that God makes knowledge about him known to humans, so that we can know and follow him. For example, many people who live in parts of the world where there is no church have reported that Jesus revealed himself to them in *dreams*. Others believe that God has spoken to them in *visions* or *impressions* to give some specific direction in their lives. *Jesus* is of course the ultimate source of Specific Revelation, not only by telling us the way, but by being the way to God. Finally, *the Bible* is our most accessible source of Specific Revelation, teaching us who God is, why we exist, and how we can know and follow him.

The Bible

The Protestant Bible is composed of 66 books which were written by many authors from several cultures over a long period of time. The Old Testament was written in Hebrew. Its story spans from Eden to a few hundred years before Jesus lived. The New Testament was written in Greek. It starts at the birth of Jesus and extends to the first years of the church. Christians universally recognized the compilation of the Bible as completed within 400 years of the resurrection. Archaeology has demonstrated that the text of the Bible has been remarkably well preserved throughout the centuries. Therefore, we have reliable manuscripts of almost the entire Bible in their original languages. Most of our English Bibles are direct translations from the original language texts and faithfully relay to us what was written by the original authors.

Although the Bible is comprised of many books, it is extraordinarily cohesive, telling one overarching story: God is at work redeeming the earth and all that is in it through Jesus Christ. From the first book, "Genesis," to the last, "Revelation," the gospel message is the central concern of the entire Bible. Every character and every story either leads to or flows from the incarnation, death, resurrection, reign, and return of Christ. Therefore, when we read the Bible, we should understand and interpret it primarily through the lens of the gospel.

The Bible in its entirety is inspired by God. This means that The Holy Spirit breathed through the human authors, while preserving their individual personalities, so that what they wrote is wholly true in all that it teaches. In this way, the Bible is a unique and special book, and our highest authority with respect to knowing and following God's will.

The Bible is also a human book, containing various forms of literature such as poetry, letters, and historical accounts. Therefore, we must interpret each book consistently with the kind of literature it represents. Historical books, such as the gospels, should be understood to depict actual events, while poetry should be understood to convey truth using symbolism. For example, Psalm 19, a poem, says that the sun "rises at one end of the heavens and makes its circuit to the other." Many early Christians, not reading this symbolically, believed that the sun literally revolved around the earth. Sadly, this mistake detracted from the truth of the gospel revealed in this Psalm: God's love. By describing the sun's motion from the observer's point of view, the poet placed humans at the very center of God's love, which is revealed through the grandeur of the heavens.

To understand poetic portions of the Bible symbolically does not mean that we understand them to be untrue. Although it may be scientifically inaccurate to say that the sun revolves around the earth, this no way infers that the Psalm is any less true. It is true because it perfectly communicates what The Holy Spirit intended to reveal: God's love for us.

Is the Bible Completely Accurate?

Accuracy in general is a difficult, if not impossible, standard to meet. For example, most timepieces, including the most sophisticated chronometers used in space, have some degree of inaccuracy. This is not necessarily a problem, however, because achieving accuracy is not always essential to accomplish one's purposes. For example, although a wrist watch is certainly not accurate enough to guide a Mars probe, it is sufficiently precise to alert one that it is lunch time. Therefore, rather than speak of *accuracy*, it is better to speak of *sufficient precision*. Like a watch, the Bible is not always completely accurate, but it is sufficiently precise for its purposes. Consider 1 Kings 7, a passage which describes the rim of a bowl to have a 10 cubit (a unit of length) diameter and a 30 cubit circumference. Given the value of π, however, a bowl with a 10 cubit diameter has a 31.4 cubit circumference. Although 30 cubits is certainly not accurate, this value is *sufficiently precise* for the intent of the author. This is because the purpose of this passage was simply to give a general historical record of the contents of the king's palace, not to create blueprints to construct a bowl. Most importantly, this inaccuracy in no way diminishes the overall message of the gospel and redemption in the Bible.

Truth

Truth Exists Outside of the Bible: Although the Bible is wholly true, it does not contain the totality of truth that exists in the universe. There is much truth, whether known or yet to be discovered, that is not written in the Bible. Science, mathematics, and history are all examples of disciplines that reveal truths to humanity that are meant to result in our benefit and well-being.

All Truth is Equally Valid: This means that one truth can't be more or less true than another. For example, consider these two statements: "Two plus two equals four" and "George Washington was the first president of the United States." These are both true statements. It is nonsensical to say that one is more or less true than the other; they are both simply true at the same time. So if science reveals a truth that seems to contradict a teaching of the Bible, we should not automatically assume that either the scientific statement or the Bible is less true. We must instead work to find a solution to uphold both truths. For example, when Galileo looked into his telescope in the seventeenth century and observed that the sun, not the earth, is the center of the solar system, it seemed to contradict the Bible. The response of church leaders at the time was to simply say that the Bible is truer than science, so Galileo must be mistaken. Galileo responded by pointing out that his discovery did not mean that the Bible was incorrect, but that the common interpretation of it was. The solution was to understand Psalm 19 as poetry that explains the *meaning* of the heavens, describing their purpose, and to understand science, by way of Galileo's observations, as explaining the *manner* of the heavens, describing how they work.

Various Truths Answer Different Questions: Reality encompasses both material and immaterial, but science can only measure and predict within the material. Science, therefore, is limited in that although it can tell us *what is* and *how it came to be*, it cannot tell us *why it is*. The Bible is also limited, in that it does not contain scientific data. So, in order to more fully comprehend reality and effectively represent God on Earth, we need a comprehensive approach to gaining knowledge that affirms both truth from the Bible and from other disciplines such as science and history. We must not pit one truth against another, but instead use the minds God gave us to arrive at solutions when truths seem to contradict. When solutions do not seem immediately apparent, we must not force resolution. Instead, we should patiently allow life's mysteries to be revealed in due time as knowledge progresses.

All Truth Is God's Truth: God is truth, and the source of all truth. He is the creator, so to observe the universe is to observe God's work. Therefore, truths correctly derived from various disciplines will inform each other. For example, well executed science can inform the Bible. Pastors are better able to help their parishioners because of what we have learned about human behavior through the discipline of psychology. This can work in the other direction as well, as the Bible can inform social science by lending insights as to why humans respond in certain ways. As humans made in the image of God, we are free to continue our quest for truth, for the more we learn, the better we will be able to know and serve God.

Summary

- General Revelation means that God made his existence known to all people through various aspects of the physical universe.
- Specific Revelation refers to particular ways in which God reveals his nature, will, and purpose, such as *dreams*, *visions*, *the person of Jesus*, and *the Bible*.
- The Bible has been reliably transmitted and translated so that we have a faithful representation of what was originally written by its authors.
- The entire Bible tells one overarching story: the gospel.
- The Bible is inspired, meaning that it is wholly true in all that it teaches.
- The Bible contains human forms of literature and must be interpreted consistently with the literary style of each passage.
- Symbolic language in the Bible is not less true than other forms of biblical literature.
- The Bible is all true, but not all that is true.
- The Bible, although not always fully accurate, is sufficiently precise for its purposes.
- All truth is equally valid, meaning that no one truth is more or less true than another.
- Truths correctly derived from various disciplines answer different questions but will not contradict.
- All truth is God's truth, meaning that truths derived from various disciplines will inform each other and help us serve God.

For Discussion

> *Please be sure to listen intently without interrupting and ask each other questions in order to gain understanding. Respond with validation, even when disagreeing. At all times strive to maintain respect for one another's point of view.*

1. Please take some time as a group to share and discuss what you underlined and why.
2. Can you relate to being especially mindful or aware of God's presence through your physical surroundings? What are the barriers to experiencing him in this way?
3. How is the claim that the Bible is inspired meaningful to you?
4. Do you think that the proposition that the Bible is a human book affects its credibility? Why or why not?
5. Do you believe that the claim that all truths are equally valid diminishes the authority of the Bible? Why or why not?
6. In what ways have you observed science and the Bible pitted against each other? What, in your mind, are the solutions to these conflicts?

For Further Study

- Psalm 19: In this poem, the author discusses, among other important truths, how God is known through his physical creation.
- 2 Timothy 3:10–17: In this letter to Timothy, his protégé pastor, Paul discusses the importance of scripture in the lives of followers of Jesus.

Chapter Seven: The Church

"It is not the church that has a mission of salvation to
fulfil in the world; it is the mission of the Son and the
Spirit through The Father that includes
the church." –Jürgen Moltmann

The pastor stood quietly after worship service,
surveying the rows of previously occupied chairs in
the empty sanctuary. Even though it had seemed like a
great morning, something was bothering him. He turned
to his wife and asked, "Hon, if you were an alien from
outer space with no prior knowledge of Earth and came
into this empty room for the first time, what would you
guess was the purpose of it just by looking at the way it is
set up?"

"Well, I would say it is a place where a bunch of
people come to hear the same information at the same
time and then go home."

"I agree," he sighed. "Sometimes, I feel like nothing
more than a well-paid Bible teacher. But I think Jesus had
much more than that in mind for us and for the church."

1. In what ways are you able to relate to this pastor's
   frustration regarding the church?
2. In what ways do you think God wants more for the
   church? What do you think might be missing?

> *Please read the article below, underlining any points that you wish to bring up later. This can be something that is especially meaningful or significant to you, something with which you agree or disagree, or something that needs further explanation.*

Is the primary purpose of church found somewhere in the relationship between the platform and the congregation? Is church more than programs that we attend once or twice a week? In this chapter, we will propose that the nature of the church is not an institution with weekly meetings, but an organism with a mission. The church is a community of people whom God sends to be the visible and tangible expression of the person of Jesus Christ in the world. Simply put, church is not something we attend, it is *who we are.*

What Is the Church?

In the Old Testament, God indwelled a room in the temple called "The Holy of Holies." Once a year, the High Priest was allowed to enter this room to make an offering for the sins of the people. At the very moment that Jesus broke the power of sin once and for all on the cross, the curtain at the entrance of The Holy of Holies was torn in two, showing that all believers now have direct access to God's abiding presence always, not just one priest once a year. Rather than indwelling a building, God now indwells his people, who form a new temple. Therefore, the church is not a building, an institution, or a corporation. The church is the totality of followers of Jesus in the world within whom God dwells. This is called the "universal church." Local churches are smaller gatherings of believers. God promised that wherever and whenever believers are gathered, he is in our midst.

Jesus is the head of the church and rules from the right hand of God. Just as Jesus carried out the mission that The Father sent him to accomplish on earth, the church, as the visible expression of Jesus in the world, is now likewise sent to fulfill God's mission on earth. Jesus has commissioned the church and given us his authority to "make disciples of all nations." The word "nations" means ethnicities, or people groups. This means that the church is called to lead people of every race to be followers of Jesus who also engage in God's mission.

Missio Dei

Missio Dei is Latin for "The Mission of God." God's mission is to redeem the earth and all that is within it through Jesus Christ, and in doing so, establish the Kingdom of God on earth. The very nature of the church is to be sent on mission. So, to be a "missional church" means to recognize and engage in *Missio Dei*. We are to join God in bringing about the Kingdom of God in the present as we anticipate God establishing his kingdom once and for all in the future when Jesus returns. The amazing result of this is that the church becomes the present revelation of the Kingdom of God on earth.

The church reveals the Kingdom of God through transformation – both by being transformed as we *encounter* God's indwelling presence as his living temple, and by being agents of transformation as we *extend* his presence as the Body of Christ to the world.

Encountering the Life-Changing Presence of Jesus Together

The earliest depictions of Christian worship show that Christians first gathered around a table for a community meal. This demonstrates their understanding that God designed his people to grow by sharing our lives together in authentic, gospel-centered community. The effects of the gospel are communal. Since God indwells the gathering of his people, we encounter him in and through each other and are thereby transformed by his presence. We become channels of God's grace in each other's lives, resulting in both individuals and entire communities of people being transformed.

The activities during a church gathering are all meant to help center our community around the gospel. *Prayer* demonstrates our dependence on God. *Musical worship* connects our intellects, emotions, and wills to our source of life in a deeper way. *Baptism* with water is how new followers of Jesus make their faith public. *Communion* is a tangible way of communicating the gospel message. *Preaching* helps us to understand the Bible and obey God. We are also called to meet each other's needs, help heal those with physical and emotional injuries, work to reconcile conflict and broken relationships, sustain each other through trials, and guide one another in difficult decisions. Above all, we must live in love and unity with each other, for this is how the world will recognize followers of Jesus.

The leadership that God wants for the church is based on its communal nature. Since Jesus is the head of the church, and since all of God's people have direct access to him, the purpose of church leadership is to empower God's people to function as a community as he intended. Rather than "top down," authoritarian leadership from one person, God calls for the church to be led by a group of humble servant-leaders who equip God's people to love and serve each other and to be on mission. The response of God's people to this leadership should be to serve in the church by contributing our time, resources, gifts, and abilities.

Extending the Life-Changing Presence of Jesus Together

Encountering Jesus in our gatherings is not an end unto itself. Rather, we are transformed so that we can be agents of transformation. Since God indwells the church, we extend the life-changing presence of Jesus wherever we go. We previously learned that through his incarnation (coming in the flesh), Jesus made the invisible God visible. Now that Jesus has ascended into heaven and is seated on his throne, the Bible calls the church "The Body of Christ." So, as his body, we continue the work of Jesus through *incarnational ministry*. This means that we are sent to extend his redeeming presence into the world. We represent him by working toward the transformation of both *people* and *places* through the gospel.

Transformation of People: To be incarnational, we must leave the confines of our physical church building and together enter into the lives of the people in our communities, develop meaningful friendships, and seek to truly be a benefit to those around us. As God provides occasions, we should graciously share the hope of the gospel that is within us, for only the power of the gospel can truly transform people. We also should invite people to belong in our church gatherings even before they believe, allowing them to encounter at their own pace the power of the gospel as it transforms the lives of his followers.

Transformation of Places: Sin's effects extend beyond individuals to institutions and places, resulting in unjust societal systems and environmental damage. Since the gospel works to renew all things, as a church we should be on mission to bring about the renewal of places in the here and now as we anticipate their ultimate renewal when Jesus returns. We accomplish this through engagement in social justice, seeking transformation of unjust structures in society that keep people oppressed, marginalized, enslaved, and poor. This work is a true expression of the gospel, which Jesus said is "good news to the poor." We should also engage in environmental justice, working to protect and restore our environment as we reclaim our vocation as God's representatives on earth.

Ethnic Diversity and *Missio Dei*

Fundamental to the nature of the kingdom is ethnic diversity. God, in some special way, designed his church so that his kingdom is revealed to the earth when people from every tribe and language worship together as one. This does not mean that we homogenize or diminish the richness and beauty that diverse cultures bring, but that we allow ourselves to be shaped and benefited by each other as the gospel acts as a reconciling force in the church and world. Ultimately, the Kingdom of God will be revealed when all nations are redeemed by God and live and serve him together for eternity. In the meantime, local congregations should strive to portray in the here and now what will be finalized in the future.

In conclusion, God's people are the new temple in which his presence dwells. We are transformed as we encounter him in community and extend his presence as the Body of Christ in the world. The church is the context in which we reclaim our vocation as image bearers of God to bring about his kingdom of love, justice, and mercy to the entire earth.

Summary

- The church is not comprised of weekly meetings or programs; it is a community of people who follow Jesus.
- God's presence indwells the church.
- The "universal church" means the totality of believers in the world.
- The Kingdom of God is by nature multi-ethnic.
- God's mission is to redeem the earth and all that is within it through Jesus Christ.
- The church is sent by God to fulfill his mission, just as Jesus did.
- The church reveals the Kingdom of God through transformation, as both an *object* and as an *agent* of transformation.
- God's people are designed to experience spiritual growth in community as we encounter God through our relationships with each other.
- The unity of God's people is the most important expression of the gospel in the church.
- The purpose of church leadership is to humbly serve God's people by equipping them to fulfill his mission.
- Incarnational ministry means that we must together leave our physical church building and extend the

presence of Jesus into our communities as we love and serve there.

- We should allow people to belong before they believe in our churches so that they can experience the life-changing presence of Jesus in our midst.

- The church also ought to engage in social and environmental justice efforts, which are valid and necessary expressions of the gospel.

For Discussion

Please be sure to listen intently without interrupting and ask each other questions in order to gain understanding. Respond with validation, even when disagreeing. At all times strive to maintain respect for one another's point of view.

1. Please take some time as a group to share and discuss what you underlined and why.

2. What are the implications of the claim that all followers of Jesus, not just one leader, have direct access to God?

3. How does the fact that all believers in the world form one church inform the concepts of nationalism and patriotism?

4. What are some obstacles to being a truly ethnically inclusive church where people are open to being shaped by each other?

5. In what ways does *Missio Dei* relate to your own personal vocation, goals, and lifestyle?

6. In your opinion, how does modern church ministry compare to that of the ancient church? What are the advantages and disadvantages of each?

7. In what ways can churches provide environments where we can effectively facilitate each other's spiritual growth? In what ways might churches unintentionally hinder that goal?

8. What are some practical ways to be agents of transformation and together bring God's presence into the world?

9. What are some practical ways to help people belong before they believe in our church gatherings? What things might be a hindrance to this goal?

For Further Study

- Acts 2:1–47: In this historical account, we first see people from all ethnicities encountering The Holy Spirit. We then encounter Peter preaching a sermon that includes most of the elements of the gospel message discussed in Chapter 3 of this book. Finally, we find an example of the communal nature of the early church.

- Revelation 7:9–17: Revelation is "apocalyptic" literature, which uses symbols and vivid imagery to communicate themes such as judgment and redemption. In this section, The Apostle John foresees God finishing his work of redemption, which includes a gathering of people from every ethnicity.

MISSIONAL UNIVERSITY
SERVICE IN THE MISSION OF GOD

Missional University helps Christian believers make a greater impact in their churches, organizations and communities through education that is rooted in the mission of God in this world. This university is redefining how Christian laypeople and clergy professionals learn through an engaging online classroom where volunteer missional leaders can maximize their giftedness and professional ministers can update their craft while preparing for the next steps in their calling. Students connect with expert faculty members from around the world who are ministry practitioners with missional experience and expertise. Missional University currently is home to the Missional College, the School of Missional Practice, the School of Community Ministry, the School of Creative Expression, the School of Ecological Mission, and the School of Theological Studies.

For more information on Missional University, or to apply, visit missional.university.

Follow Us

Made in the USA
San Bernardino, CA
20 November 2017